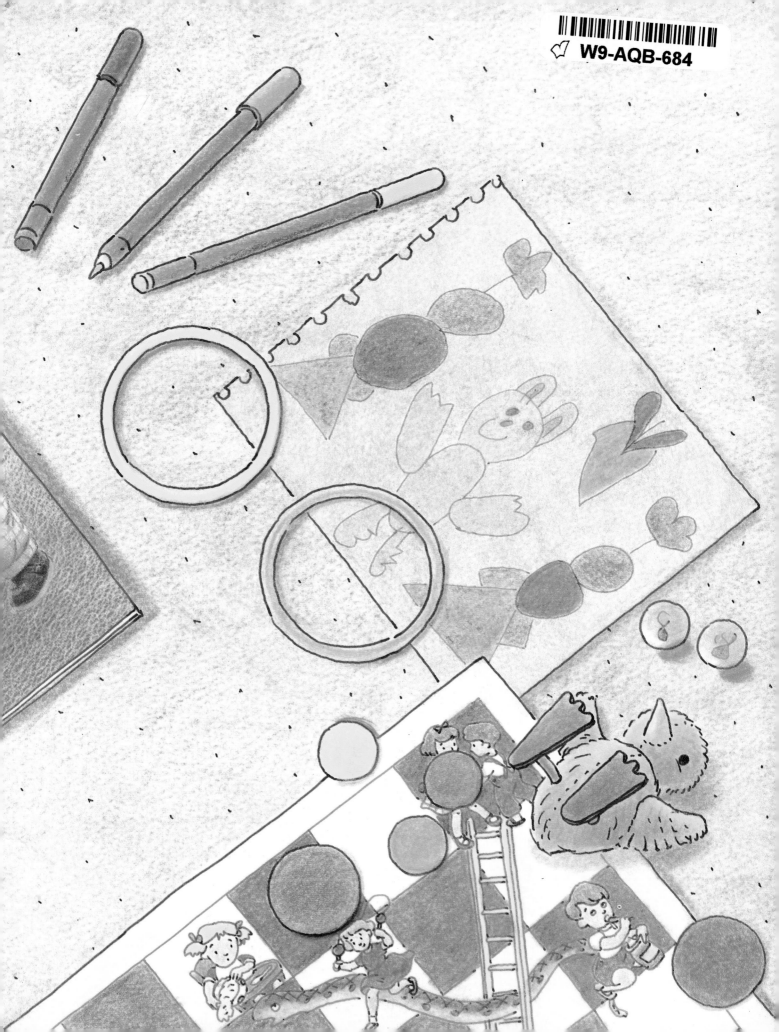

First Questions and Answers about the **Human Body**

# What Is a Bellybutton?

TIME LIFE *for* Children ®

ALEXANDRIA, VIRGINIA

# Contents

# Why do I get hungry?

When you feel hungry or your stomach grumbles, your body is telling you it's time to eat!

Your body is like a car. A car needs gas
to make it go. Your body needs gas, too.
The food you eat is gas for your body.

# What happens to the food I eat?

Food takes a long trip through your body.

1. The trip begins in your mouth. Your teeth chew the food into tiny pieces so it is easy to swallow.

2. The chewed food goes down a tube to your stomach. Your stomach mixes together everything, from apples to peanut butter.

6

3. Then the food moves through another tube called the intestine. As the food moves through the intestine, your body takes out the parts it can use.

4. The parts of the food your body can't use stay in the tube and travel all the way to its end. They come out when you go to the bathroom.

# Why do I have to brush my teeth?

Not all the food you eat goes to your stomach. A few small pieces stick to your teeth. If the food stays there too long, it can cause your teeth to get tiny holes, called cavities. Brushing your teeth washes away the food before cavities can form.

**Did you know?**

The first teeth you have are called baby teeth. When you are five or six years old, they begin to fall out one by one, and a new set of grown-up teeth takes their place.

# Why do I have to put on sunscreen?

Sunscreen protects your skin. Warm sun feels good, but too much of it hurts your skin. You could get a stinging sunburn. Sunscreen helps stop the sunlight from burning your skin.

**Did you know?**

People with fair, or light, skin tend to burn faster than people with dark skin.

11

# Why do my friend and I have different skin colors?

Your skin has tiny bits of color in it, called melanin. People with lots of melanin have dark skin. People with a little melanin have light skin.

People come in many different colors. Although our bodies are different colors on the outside, inside they are all the same.

# Why do I breathe faster when I run?

You suck in air through your nose and mouth, day and night. That's called breathing. Your body needs air for walking, talking, playing, and thinking. When you run fast, your body works extra hard. You need extra air, so you breathe faster.

# Why do I sweat when I am hot?

Sweating cools you off. As you exercise, or when it's hot outside, your body heats up. When you get too hot, you sweat. Sweat is salty water. As your skin dries, the water goes into the air. It takes some heat along, so you feel cooler.

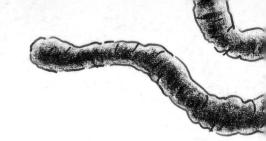

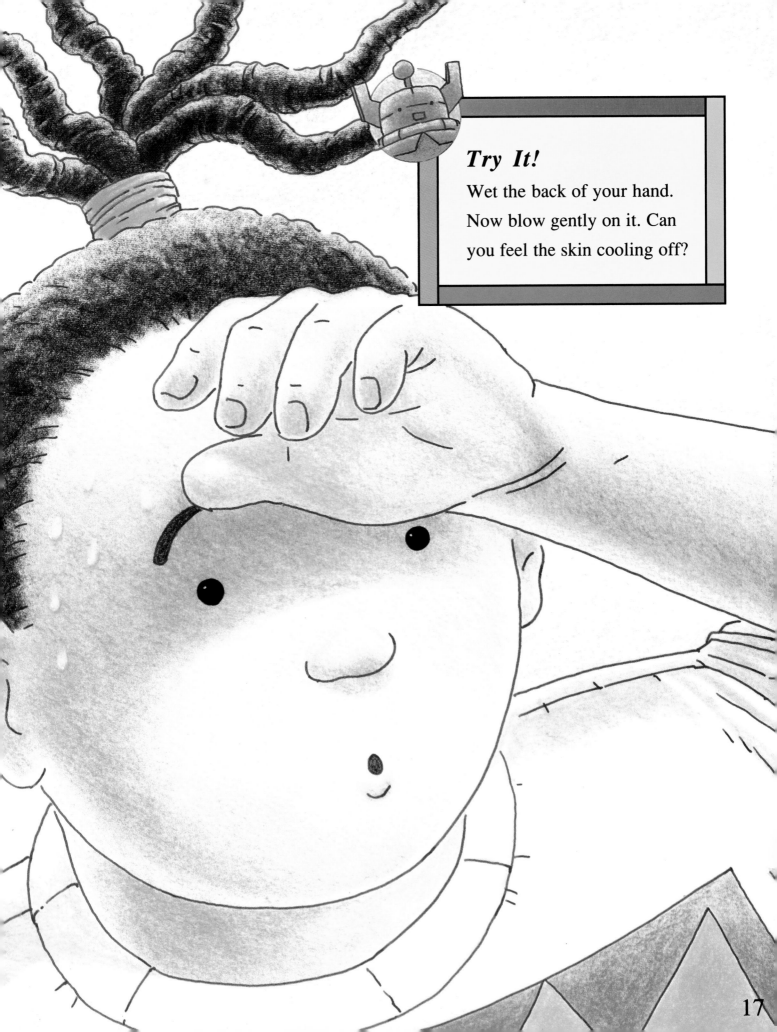

**Try It!**

Wet the back of your hand. Now blow gently on it. Can you feel the skin cooling off?

17

# What makes my arms and legs so strong?

Your arms and legs have muscles in them. So do other parts of your body. Muscles make your body move—and they make you strong. You use them to walk, hop, and jump. You also use them to stick out your tongue, wiggle your fingers, and blink your eyes.

**Did you know?**
When you smile, you are using
15 different muscles in your face!

19

# Why do I bleed when I cut myself?

Your blood travels through tubes in your body called blood vessels. When you scratch or cut your skin, you also break some tiny blood vessels just under the skin. That's why blood trickles out.

**Did you know?**

Your body can fix most small cuts by itself. When you bleed, the blood dries and forms a scab. Under that scab, the skin is healing. When it is all better, the scab falls off.

# Why do I have to go to the doctor?

Your body can fix small things like cuts by itself. But sometimes if you are hurt or sick you need to visit the doctor. A doctor also sees you when you are not sick. She makes sure you are healthy. Here are some things the doctor does:

She measures and weighs you to see how you've grown.

She listens to your heart, which pumps blood through your body. She also listens to your lungs, which help you breathe.

She looks inside your eyes, ears, and mouth.

*Here's where your heart and lungs are.*

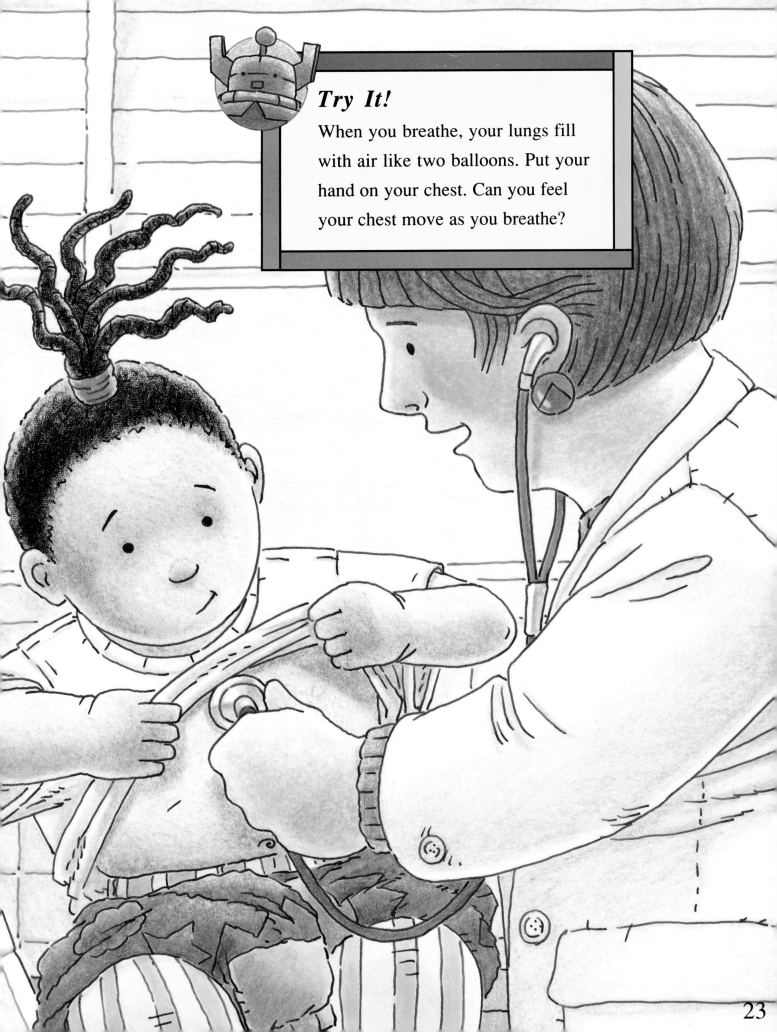

**Try It!**

When you breathe, your lungs fill with air like two balloons. Put your hand on your chest. Can you feel your chest move as you breathe?

23

# Why do I have to get a shot if I don't feel sick?

Shots protect you from germs. Germs are too small to see, but they are everywhere. When germs get inside us, they can make us feel sick.

When you get a shot, your body makes germ fighters. They protect you from some of the germs that could make you sick.

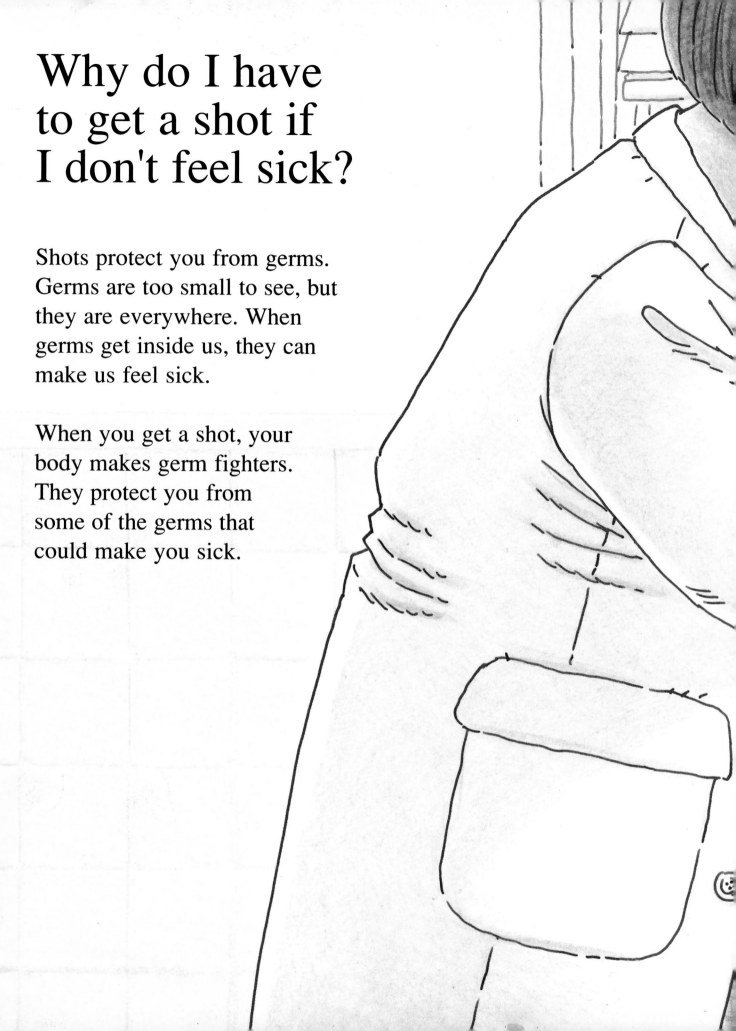

# Why do loud noises hurt my ears?

Every noise travels through the air to your ear. When a sound reaches your ear, it makes tiny parts move inside your ear. The moving parts help you figure out what the sound is and how loud it is. A really loud noise makes the tiny parts move a lot, which can hurt.

# What happens when you break a bone?

Your bones are hard and strong, but if you have a bad fall a bone can crack or break. Then a doctor puts a cast over the broken place. A cast is like a hard shell that holds the broken bone in place. Slowly, the broken pieces grow together. Once the bone heals, the cast comes off.

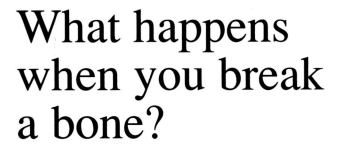

*An x-ray picture shows what your bones look like inside you.*

### Did you know?
You have over 206 bones in your body. Together they are called your skeleton.

# Why does bright light make me squint?

Your eyes use light to help you see. But too much light all of a sudden will make you squint. On a normal day it's brighter outside than inside. When you walk outside, light rushes into your eye. You squeeze your eyes shut to block that extra light.

KING ROO

KIN

**_Did you know?_**

In the center of each eye is a black circle, called the pupil. Your pupils change size to let the right amount of light into your eyes.

When it is dark out, your pupils get bigger.

When it is bright out, they get smaller.

LIBRARY

Green fingers

Green fingers

SNIPS

SNIPS

# Why do some people wear glasses?

Your eye sees just like a movie camera. And like a camera, each eye has a curved part called a lens. A lens helps you see clearly. But some eyes have lenses that don't work right, and they see pictures that are fuzzy and out of focus. Glasses also have lenses in them. They help eyes see clear pictures.

### Did you know?

Many people who wear glasses don't need them all the time. Some wear them only to help them see things far away. Others, like Teddy, wear glasses to see things close to them, like a book.

Without glasses, Teddy's book looks like this to him.

With glasses, it looks like this.

# Why doesn't it hurt when you get a haircut?

Hair is not like skin. It cannot feel things. So when someone cuts hair, it doesn't hurt at all. Each hair grows from a root in the skin. When someone pulls your hair, he or she tugs on the skin. Your skin can feel pain, so it hurts.

### Did you know?

If you look closely, you will find hair all over your body. You have hair everywhere except the palms of your hands, the bottoms of your feet, and your lips.

# Why do I sneeze?

A sneeze clears your nose. When you breathe in, tiny hairs inside your nose keep out things like dirt and dust. Sometimes the dirt or dust gets past these hairs into your nose, and you feel a tickle. This makes you sneeze.

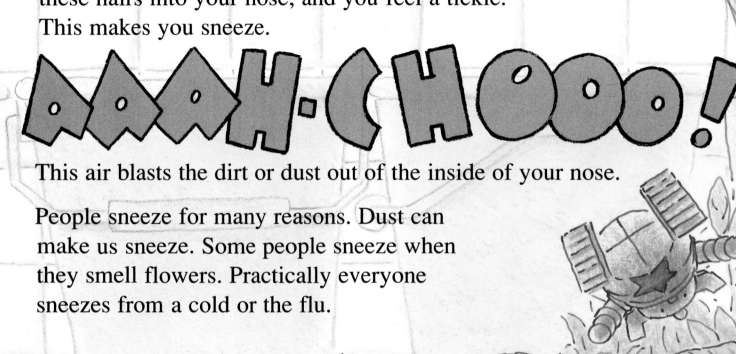

This air blasts the dirt or dust out of the inside of your nose.

People sneeze for many reasons. Dust can make us sneeze. Some people sneeze when they smell flowers. Practically everyone sneezes from a cold or the flu.

# Why don't things taste good when my nose is stuffy?

Tasting and smelling go together. When you bite a chocolate-chip cookie, you can smell it too. That wonderful smell makes it taste even better.

When you have a cold, your stuffy nose can't smell very well. So things you eat don't taste as good as they usually do.

39

# Why am I ticklish?

There are millions of places under your skin that send your brain a message when something touches you. These places are called nerves. Nerves tell your brain whether something is hot or cold, hard or soft, or fluffy or scratchy. When someone tickles you, your brain sends a message back: Laugh! or Pull away!

### Did you know?

It doesn't tickle when you tickle yourself.
Only another person can give you that nice
tickly feeling. Try it and see.

41

# Why do I get hiccups?

Hiccups are caused by a kind of tickle inside you. Just above your stomach are some muscles. These muscles move in and out slowly as you breathe. When something bothers them—like a lot of laughing, a surprise, or eating too much or too fast—the muscles move in short sudden bursts. Those are hiccups.

Here are some ways to get rid of hiccups.

1. Drink a big glass of water.

2. Take a deep breath and hold it as long as you can.

# What is a bellybutton?

Before you were born, you grew inside your mother.
Even though you couldn't eat, you needed food.

A baby and its mother are connected by a cord. Food
goes to the baby from its mother through this cord.
When a baby is born, it can eat for itself. It doesn't
need the cord anymore, so the doctor cuts the cord off.
All that is left is one tiny spot. That's the bellybutton.

*Some bellybuttons poke out
and some are pulled in.
Which kind do you have?*

# Why can't fathers have babies?

Mothers and fathers make babies together. But only mothers have a place inside them where babies can grow. The place is called a uterus. It takes about nine months for a baby to grow inside its mother's uterus.

## TIME-LIFE for CHILDREN®

**President:** Robert H. Smith
**Associate Publisher/Managing Editor:** Neil Kagan
**Assistant Managing Editor:** Patricia Daniels
**Editorial Directors:** Jean Burke Crawford, Allan Fallow,
Karin Kinney, Sara Mark, Elizabeth Ward
**Director of Marketing:** Margaret Mooney
**Product Managers:** Cassandra Ford, Amy Haworth,
Shelley L. Schimkus
**Director of Finance:** Lisa Peterson
**Publishing Assistant:** Marike van der Veen
**Administrative Assistant:** Barbara A. Jones
**Production Manager:** Marlene Zack
**Senior Copyeditor:** Colette Stockum
**Production:** Celia Beattie
**Supervisor of Quality Control:** James King
**Library:** Louise D. Forstall
**Special Contributor:** Barbara Klein
**Researcher:** Joann S. Stern
**Writer:** Andrew Gutelle

**Designed by:** **David Bennett Books**

**Series design:** David Bennett
**Book design:** Andrew Crowson
**Art direction:** David Bennett & Andrew Crowson
**Illustrated by:** Clive Scruton
**Additional cover**
**illustrations by:** Malcolm Livingstone

First printing. Printed in U.S.A.
Published simultaneously in Canada.

Time Life Inc. is a wholly owned subsidiary of THE TIME INC. BOOK COMPANY.

TIME-LIFE is a trademark of Time Warner Inc. U.S.A.

For subscription information, call 1-800-621-7026.

**Library of congress Cataloging-in-Publication Data**

What is a Bellybutton? : first questions and answers about the human body.
p. cm.— ( Time-Life library of first questions and answers)
Summary : Answers questions about the human body, such as "Why do I
get hungry?" and "Why do I breathe faster when I run?"
ISBN 0-7835-0854-9.— ISBN 0-7835-0855-7 (lib. bdg.)
1. Body, Human — Juvenile literature. [ 1.Body, Human —
Miscellanea. 2. Human physiology —.Miscellanea. 3.Questions and
answers.] I Time-Life for Children (Firm) II.Series: Library of
first questions and answers.
QP37.W43 1993
612 — dc20
93-6654
CIP
AC

**Consultants**

**Dr. Lewis P. Lipsitt**, an internationally recognized specialist on childhood development, was the 1990 recipient of the Nicholas Hobbs Award for science in the service of children. He has served as the science director for the American Psychological Association and is a professor of psychology and medical science at Brown University, where he is director of the Child Study Center.

**Dr. Judith A. Schickedanz**, an authority on the education of preschool children, is an associate professor of early childhood education at the Boston University School of Education, where she also directs the Early Childhood Learning Laboratory. Her published work includes *More Than the ABC's: Early Stages of Reading and Writing Development* as well as several textbooks and many scholarly papers.

What Is a Bellybutton?

First Questions and Answers about the Human Body

AUG 1994